# *Essential* COOKING SERIES

## COMPREHENSIVE, STEP-BY-STEP COOKING

# Grilling &
# Barbecuing

HINKLER
BOOKS

Essential Cooking Series: Grilling & Barbecuing
First published in 2009 by Hinkler Books Pty Ltd
45–55 Fairchild Street
Heatherton Victoria 3202 Australia
www.hinklerbooks.com

Disclaimer: The nutritional information listed under each recipe does not
include the nutrient content of garnishes or any accompaniments not listed
in specific quantitites in the ingredient list. The nutritional information for
each recipe is an estimate only, and may vary depending on the brand of
ingredients used, and due to natural biological variations in the composition
of natural foods such as meat, fish, fruit and vegetables. The nutritional
information was calculated by using Foodworks dietary analysis software
(Version 3, Xyris Software Pty Ltd, Highgate Hill, Queensland, Australia) based
on the Australian food composition tables and food manufacturers' data.
Where not specified, ingredients are always analysed as average or medium,
not small or large.

ISBN: 978 1 7418 5714 6

10 9 8 7 6 5 4 3 2
14 13 12 11 10

Printed and bound in China

# Contents

# An introduction to grilling and barbecuing

A balmy summer's day, a few good friends, a glass of wine and the aroma of cooking food – there's nothing quite like a barbecue. It can be as simple as a few sausages served with crusty bread and a fresh green salad or as fancy as an outdoor dinner party serving seafood kebabs, marinated lamb cutlets, chargrilled vegetable stacks and whole pieces of meat. Whatever the occasion, this book has exciting recipes that will impress.

## SAFETY

A safe barbecue is a fun barbecue. Clear a space for your barbecue, away from any bush or combustible material. If you have a balcony or backyard, set up your barbecue in a corner and make sure not to push it up against a wall, as the heat can burn nearby surfaces.

If using a gas barbecue with a drip tray, line the tray with sand to prevent dripping fat from igniting. If your barbecue does not have an automatic ignition, purchase long matches or a gas lighter. The utensils you use when cooking on a barbecue are important; barbecue shops sell long-handled tongs that will make turning food easy.

If there are young children in the gathering, be sure to keep them well away from the cooking area. Brightly coloured kettle/weber barbecues are often tempting for little fingers. Keep a close eye on the kids, and don't leave a hot barbecue unsupervised.

Never pour flammable liquid onto a barbecue to start it or to increase the heat.

## TYPES OF BARBECUES

There are many barbecues available on the market. The main varieties are fuel burning, and gas or electric.

FUEL BURNING FIXED BARBECUES: Fixed barbecues are usually built to a simple design in backyards, parks and picnic grounds. They are constructed with bricks or cement and have a flat plate and chargrill. A wood fire is built under the plates and left to burn until the coals are hot. The disadvantage: they can't be moved in bad weather.

KETTLE/WEBER BARBECUES: Increasingly popular over the years, kettle/weber barbecues come in a variety of sizes and are perfect for people living in units. They are portable and can be taken on holidays or to a park. They cook as an open barbecue, a smoker or a kettle oven.

BRAZIER: Braziers are simple, small and portable barbecues consisting of a box for fuel and a grill for cooking. Some braziers have lids that help the food cook evenly.

**GAS OR ELECTRIC BARBECUES:** Easy to use and ready at a moment's notice, gas or electric barbecues are the most popular barbecues. These barbecues use trays of volcanic rock, which are heated with either electricity or gas, and a flat plate and chargrill above the rocks. Usually mounted into timber stands, they often come with hoods that allow for even cooking and protection from the elements.

## SOURCE OF HEAT
### Wood
Lighting a wood fire can be tricky on a windy day. It can also be difficult if the wood is slightly damp or green. Gather blends of kindling to start the fire and slowly increase the size of the pieces of wood as the fire gathers heat. Don't be tempted to start cooking over a raging fire. Allow the fire time to burn down until you are left with a nice bed of hot coals. By this time your barbecue

plate will be heated and ready for you to cook. Remember to keep stoking the fire.

## Charcoal, heat beads and barbecue briquettes

Charcoal, heat beads or barbecue briquettes are a widely used source of fuel for kettle/weber barbecues or braziers. They are easy to use and produce a reliable, constant source of heat. They are available from supermarkets or barbecue shops. To light them you will need to use firelighters, which are usually sold beside the heatbeads in the supermarket. Firelighters should only be used to light the beads, and not to keep a fire going. No cooking should commence until the firelighters have finished burning, as they have been soaked in kerosene and give off an unpleasant aroma that can easily permeate the food. Don't be heavy-handed with firelighters. It's best to read the manufacturer's instructions but as a general guide, 2–3 firelighters will ignite roughly 20 beads. Allow the fire to burn

until the beads turn white. This will take approximately 40 minutes. After handling the charcoal and firelighters, make sure you wash your hands before handling the food.

## Gas or Electricity

Gas barbecues are either fuelled with a gas bottle or connected to a gas main. Electric barbecues can be connected to an electricity supply. A dial at the front of the barbecue controls the temperature.

### COOKING

There are two ways of barbecuing food – direct and indirect. Direct heat cooks the food directly over the flame or coals. Indirect heat applies only to kettle/weber barbecues, which have an oven-style set up.

DIRECT HEAT: To cook with direct heat is very simple. Preheat the barbecue to moderate-high, oil the grill using a long-handled pastry brush and place one piece of food onto the barbecue. The food should sizzle once it hits the hotplate: if it doesn't, remove it and allow the barbecue to continue heating. Start by searing the food on the hottest part of the barbecue; this is often towards the back. Once you have turned the food, move it to a more moderate heat and continue cooking; this will allow the food to cook evenly without burning. It is a good idea to have one part of an electric or gas barbecue turned down low, so you can keep cooked food warm while finishing off pieces of meat that take longer.

You can use the flat plate as you would an element on a stove – to reheat

marinades in a saucepan, to stir-fry or even to make pancakes.

INDIRECT HEAT: Although cooking with indirect heat is slower than cooking with direct heat, it imparts a unique flavour into the food. Light the barbecue using heat beads and firelighters. Refer to the manufacturer's instructions for the quantity of beads, which will vary according to the size of the barbecue and the amount of food being cooked.

1   Remove the lid and slide open the vent at the bottom of the kettle.

2   Put the racks into position and place the heat beads and firelighters into the side baskets. Light and leave until the beads are covered with a fine ash. Do not add any food until the beads are white.

Do not cover the barbecue until the beads are heated.

3   Place a dish in the bottom of the kettle/weber to catch any excess fat. Position the cooking rack and top with the food. Cover and cook according to the recipe.

You can also use a kettle/weber as a smoker or oven and they are wonderful for roasting large pieces of meat or cooking the Christmas ham or turkey. To smoke foods on a kettle, simply prepare the kettle as instructed above and, when the heat beads are covered in white ash, add a handful of smoking chips that have been soaked in water or wine for 30 minutes. Cover and smoke following the recipe.

# Lamb cutlets with garlic mayonnaise

## INGREDIENTS

$^1/_2$ cup (125 ml, 4 fl oz) olive oil
2 garlic cloves, crushed
2 tablespoons finely chopped parsley
1 tablespoon chopped fresh thyme
$1^1/_2$ tablespoons lemon juice
12 lamb cutlets
salt and freshly ground black pepper
*quick aïoli*
1 egg
$^3/_4$ cup (185 g, 6 oz) mayonnaise
1 tablespoon extra virgin olive oil
1 tablespoon lemon juice
4 cloves garlic, crushed
**serves 4**

PREPARATION TIME
30 minutes, plus
2 hours marinating

COOKING TIME
10 minutes

1  In a large shallow bowl, combine $^1/_2$ cup (125 ml, 4 fl oz) oil, 2 cloves garlic, parsley, thyme, and $1^1/_2$ tablespoons lemon juice. Add cutlets and coat well. Cover and refrigerate for at least 2 hours.

2  Preheat barbecue to high heat. In a small bowl, combine egg, mayonnaise and oil, lemon juice and garlic. Whisk until smooth.

3  Drain chops, reserving marinade. Cook the chops on barbecue for 2–3 minutes each side, basting occasionally with marinade. Season with salt and pepper. Serve drizzled with aïoli.

| NUTRITIONAL VALUE PER SERVE | FAT 24.8 G | CARBOHYDRATE 4.2 G | PROTEIN 12.4 G |
| --- | --- | --- | --- |

# Greek shish kebabs

## INGREDIENTS

750 g (1½ lb) lamb neck fillet,
    cut into 2.5 cm (1 in) pieces
fresh mint to garnish
lemon wedges to serve

*marinade*

100 g (3½ oz) Greek yoghurt
½ onion, grated
2 cloves garlic, crushed
juice of ½ lemon
1 tablespoon olive oil
3 tablespoons chopped fresh mint
salt and black pepper
8 small metal skewers

**makes 8**

PREPARATION TIME
20 minutes

COOKING TIME
15–20 minutes,
plus overnight or
4 hours marinating

1  Preheat barbecue to a high heat.

2  In a large bowl, combine yoghurt, onion, garlic, lemon juice,
   oil, mint and seasoning. Add lamb and toss to coat. Cover and
   refrigerate for 4 hours or overnight.

3  Thread lamb onto metal skewers. Cook kebabs on barbecue for
   10–12 minutes, turning 2–3 times, until cooked through. Garnish
   with mint and serve with lemon wedges.

| NUTRITIONAL VALUE PER SERVE | FAT 5.5 G | CARBOHYDRATE 1.5 G | PROTEIN 16.8 G |
| --- | --- | --- | --- |

# Mini lamb roast with barbecued noodles

## INGREDIENTS

1 trim lamb mini roast
2 tablespoons chopped
  fresh coriander (cilantro)
1 clove garlic, crushed
salt and pepper
1 tablespoon lemon juice
1 tablespoon oil

### Barbecued noodles

500 g (1 lb) hokkien noodles
1 tablespoon chopped
  fresh coriander (cilantro)
100 g (3½ oz) feta cheese, crumbled
1 clove garlic, crushed
½ teaspoon chopped chilli (optional)

**serves 4**

PREPARATION TIME
20 minutes, plus
1 hour marinating

COOKING TIME
40 minutes, plus
15 minutes standing

1 Preheat kettle/weber or hooded gas barbecue for indirect cooking. Tie the mini roast with kitchen string to retain moisture.

2 In a large glass bowl, combine coriander (cilantro), garlic, salt and pepper, lemon juice and oil. Place lamb into marinade and turn to coat on all sides. Marinate for 1 hour at room temperature.

3 Place lamb over drip tray in centre of barbecue, cover with lid or hood and cook for 35–40 minutes. There is no need to turn. Alternatively, place lamb in a foil tray, brushing with marinade as it cooks. Allow to stand 10–15 minutes before carving.

### Barbecued noodles

1 Rinse noodles in hot water and separate. Drain well. In a small bowl, combine coriander (cilantro), feta, garlic and chilli, mixing to a paste.

2 Heat barbecue plate to high. Lightly oil and add noodles, tossing with coriander paste. Mix well and heat through. (Alternatively, use a baking dish on the grill plate to cook the noodles.)

3 Serve carved lamb on barbecued noodles and drizzle with remaining juices if desired.

| NUTRITIONAL VALUE PER SERVE | FAT 5.0 G | CARBOHYDRATE 15.8 G | PROTEIN 16.4 G |
| --- | --- | --- | --- |

# Barbecued lamb pitta breads

### INGREDIENTS

1 tablespoon lemon finely
  grated rind (zest)
1 teaspoon ground cumin
1 tablespoon olive oil
750 g (1¹/₂ lb) lamb fillets
6 pitta bread rounds
125 g (4 oz) ready-made hummus
1 bunch endive (curly chicory)
250 g (8 oz) ready-made tabbouleh
**serves 6**

PREPARATION TIME
15 minutes, plus
30 minutes
marinating

COOKING TIME
15 minutes

1 Combine lemon rind, cumin and oil in a small bowl. Rub surface of lamb
  with oil mixture, place in a shallow glass dish and marinate at room
  temperature for 30 minutes.

2 Preheat barbecue to a medium heat. Place lamb on lightly oiled barbecue
  grill and cook for 3–5 minutes each side or until lamb is tender and cooked
  to your liking. Stand for 2 minutes before slicing.

3 Warm pitta breads on barbecue for 1–2 minutes each side. Split each pitta
  bread to make a pocket, then spread with hummus and fill with endive,
  tabbouleh and sliced lamb.

NUTRITIONAL VALUE PER SERVE       FAT **3.9** G        CARBOHYDRATE **18.8** G        PROTEIN **11.7** G

# Herbed and spiced pork loin

**INGREDIENTS**

2 kg (4 lb) boneless pork loin,
  rolled and rind scored at
  2 cm (1 in) intervals

*herb and spice marinade*

1 onion, chopped

2 tablespoons pink peppercorns,
  crushed

2 tablespoons green peppercorns,
  crushed

2 tablespoons ground coriander
  (cilantro)

1 tablespoon freshly ground
  black pepper

1 tablespoon ground cumin

1 teaspoon garam masala

1 teaspoon ground mixed spice

1 teaspoon turmeric

1 teaspoon paprika

1 teaspoon sea salt

2 tablespoons peanut oil

2 tablespoons sesame oil

1 tablespoon white vinegar

**serves 8**

1 In a food processor or blender, place onion, peppercorns, coriander, black pepper, cumin, garam masala, mixed spice, turmeric, paprika, salt, peanut oil, sesame oil and vinegar and process to a smooth paste.

2 Rub marinade over pork, place in a large glass dish, cover and refrigerate overnight.

3 Place pork on a wire rack set in a baking dish and bake at 190°C (375°F, gas mark 5) for 1 hour.

4 Preheat barbecue to a medium heat. Transfer pork to lightly oiled barbecue grill and cook, turning frequently, for 1½ hours or until pork is tender and cooked through. Stand for 15 minutes before carving and serving.

PREPARATION TIME
30 minutes, plus
overnight marinating

COOKING TIME
2½ hours, plus
15 minutes standing

| NUTRITIONAL VALUE PER SERVE | FAT 9.1 G | CARBOHYDRATE 0.4 G | PROTEIN 25.9 G |
| --- | --- | --- | --- |

# Mixed sausage and onion grill

**INGREDIENTS**

12 assorted sausages
3 red onions, quartered
olive oil
12 metal skewers
12 baby new potatoes,
  scrubbed and cooked
**serves 4–6**

1 Parboil sausages by placing in a large pan and covering with water. Bring slowly to the boil, reduce heat and simmer for 5 minutes. Drain, cool and refrigerate for several hours or overnight.

2 Preheat barbecue to a medium heat. Thread onion quarters onto six lightly oiled skewers (2 quarters on each skewer), then brush with oil. Cook on lightly oiled barbecue, turning halfway through cooking, for 15–20 minutes or until onions are golden and tender.

3 Thread potatoes onto another six lightly oiled skewers (2 potatoes on each skewer), then brush with oil. Cook on barbecue, turning halfway through cooking, for 10–15 minutes or until potatoes are golden and heated through.

4 Cook sausages on lightly oiled barbecue for 10–15 minutes or until sausages are golden and crisp on the outside and heated through.

PREPARATION TIME
20 minutes, plus
2–3 hours or overnight
refrigeration

COOKING TIME
30 minutes

| NUTRITIONAL VALUE PER SERVE | FAT 15.2 G | CARBOHYDRATE 7.4 G | PROTEIN 5.5 G |

# Perfect T-bone steak

## INGREDIENTS

4 T-bone steaks
2 cloves garlic, crushed
2 teaspoons oil
salt and pepper
*garlic butter*
4 tablespoons butter
1 clove garlic, crushed
1 tablespoon parsley flakes
2 teaspoons lemon juice
**serves 4**

1 Preheat barbecue to a high heat. Bring the steaks to room temperature. Combine garlic, oil and salt and pepper. Rub onto both sides of steak. Stand for 10–15 minutes at room temperature.

2 Sear steaks for one minute each side. Cook for 2–3 minutes each side until cooked to your liking. Total time 5–6 minutes for rare, 7–10 minutes for medium and 10–14 minutes for well done.

3 Mix all garlic butter ingredients together. Serve on top of steak.

PREPARATION TIME
**15 minutes, plus 15 minutes standing**

COOKING TIME
**6–15 minutes**

NUTRITIONAL VALUE PER SERVE    FAT **8.8** G    CARBOHYDRATE **0.2** G    PROTEIN **19.6** G

# Cheese-filled beef patties

**INGREDIENTS**

600 g (1¼ lb) lean minced beef
1 tablespoon barbecue sauce
2 tablespoons tomato sauce
1 small onion, finely chopped
60 g (2 oz) mature cheddar, grated
125 g (4 oz) can crushed pineapple,
  drained
**makes 4 large patties**

PREPARATION TIME
15 minutes

COOKING TIME
20 minutes

1  Preheat barbecue to a medium heat. In a large bowl, place beef,
   barbecue sauce, tomato sauce and onion and mix to combine.
   Shape beef mixture into 8 patties, flattening slightly with the
   palm of your hand.

2  Top 4 patties with cheese and pineapple, then cover with
   remaining patties, carefully moulding edges of patties together
   to form 4 larger patties.

3  Cook patties on lightly oiled barbecue for
   10 minutes each side.

NUTRITIONAL VALUE PER SERVE      FAT **7.1** G      CARBOHYDRATE **3.9** G      PROTEIN **15.9** G

# Warm Thai chicken salad

## INGREDIENTS

4 chicken breast fillets
2 teaspoons ready-made
  Thai-style marinade
1 teaspoon oil
1 red capsicum (pepper),
  deseeded and cut into strips
1 green capsicum (pepper), deseeded
  and cut into strips
1 aubergine (eggplant), sliced
1 red onion, cut into rings
½ cos (romaine) lettuce, shredded
*dressing*
4 tablespoons malt vinegar
½ cup (125 ml, 4 fl oz) olive oil
extra teaspoon ready-made
  Thai-style marinade
**serves 4**

1 Flatten chicken breasts slightly to even
  thickness. In a small bowl, combine
  2 teaspoons Thai-style marinade and
  1 teaspoon oil and rub well into the chicken.
  Cover and stand 20 minutes before cooking.

2 Heat the barbecue to medium-high and lightly
  oil hotplate and grill bars. Place chicken on grill
  and cook 4 minutes each side. Place capsicums
  (peppers), aubergine (eggplant) and onion on
  the hotplate, drizzle with a little oil and cook
  for 5–8 minutes, tossing to cook through.
  Pile lettuce onto individual plates and place
  barbecued vegetables in the centre. Cut the
  chicken into thin diagonal slices and arrange
  on top of vegetables.

3 In a small bowl, combine vinegar, oil and
  Thai-style marinade and pour over chicken and
  warm salad. Serve with crusty bread.

PREPARATION TIME
**15 minutes, plus
20 minutes standing**

COOKING TIME
**15 minutes**

| NUTRITIONAL VALUE PER SERVE | FAT **8.9** G | CARBOHYDRATE **0.9** G | PROTEIN **13.8** G |

# Buffalo chilli chicken

## INGREDIENTS

1 kg (2 lb) chicken pieces, skinned
3 spring onions (green onions),
  chopped
2 cloves garlic, crushed
1 cup (250 ml, 8 fl oz) tomato sauce
4 tablespoons beer
1 tablespoon cider vinegar
1 tablespoon honey
1 tablespoon tabasco sauce
**serves 4–6**

PREPARATION TIME
20 minutes, plus
3–4 hours
marinating

COOKING TIME
10–15 minutes

**1** Score larger pieces of chicken at 2 cm (1 in) intervals and set aside.

**2** Place spring onions (green onions), garlic, tomato sauce, beer, vinegar, honey and tabasco sauce in a large shallow glass dish and mix to combine. Add chicken, toss to coat, cover and refrigerate for 3–4 hours.

**3** Preheat barbecue to a medium heat. Drain chicken and reserve marinade. Place chicken on lightly oiled barbecue grill and cook, basting frequently with reserved marinade and turning several times, for 10–15 minutes or until chicken is tender and cooked through.

NUTRITIONAL VALUE PER SERVE        FAT **5.5** G        CARBOHYDRATE **6.5** G        PROTEIN **13.5** G

# Chicken patties served on basil flapjacks with chilli yoghurt sauce

**INGREDIENTS**

*patties*

500 g (1 lb) chicken mince
1/2 teaspoon salt
1/4 teaspoon pepper
1 clove garlic, crushed
1/2 teaspoon chopped fresh chilli
2 tablespoons dried breadcrumbs
4 tablespoons water

*flapjacks*

150 g (5 oz) self-raising flour
1/4 teaspoon salt
2 tablespoons chopped fresh basil
1 clove garlic, crushed
3/4 cup (185 ml, 6 fl oz) milk
1 egg

*chilli yoghurt sauce*

200 g (7 oz) natural yoghurt
2 teaspoons sweet chilli sauce

**serves 6**

PREPARATION TIME
30 minutes,
plus 40 minutes
refrigeration

COOKING TIME
30 minutes

1 In a large bowl, combine all patty ingredients, mixing well with hands. Cover and refrigerate for 20 minutes. With wet hands, form into small flat patties about 2.5 cm (1 in) in diameter. Place on a flat tray, cover and refrigerate.

2 For the flapjacks, sift the flour and salt into a large bowl. In a separate bowl, combine the basil, garlic and milk, then beat in the egg. Make a well in the centre of the flour and pour in the milk mixture. Stir to form a smooth batter. Cover and set aside for 20 minutes.

3 Heat barbecue until hot and lightly oil the grill bars and hotplate. Brush the patties with a little oil and place on grill bars. Grill for 2 minutes each side. Pour 4 tablespoons of flapjack mixture onto the greased hotplate. Cook until bubbles appear over the surface and the bottom is golden. Flip over and cook until golden. Transfer to a clean towel and cover to keep hot. Repeat for remaining flapjacks.

4 In a small bowl, combine yoghurt and sweet chilli sauce. Serve flapjacks topped with 3 patties and a dollop of chilli yoghurt sauce.

| NUTRITIONAL VALUE PER SERVE | FAT 5.5 G | CARBOHYDRATE 12.3 G | PROTEIN 11.9 G |
| --- | --- | --- | --- |

# Spicy mango chicken

### INGREDIENTS

4 chicken breast fillets
1 teaspoon freshly ground
    black pepper
1 teaspoon ground cumin
1 teaspoon paprika
4 slices prosciutto or ham, halved
2 mangoes, peeled and cut into
    2 cm (1 in) thick slices
*mango sauce*
1 mango, peeled and chopped
1 clove garlic, crushed
2 tablespoons golden syrup
1 tablespoon sweet chilli sauce
**serves 4**

PREPARATION TIME
20 minutes

COOKING TIME
20 minutes

**1** Preheat barbecue to high.

**2** Place chicken between sheets of greaseproof paper and pound lightly with a meat mallet to flatten to 1 cm ($^1/_4$ in) thick.

**3** Combine black pepper, cumin and paprika and sprinkle over chicken. Layer prosciutto or ham and mango slices on chicken, roll up and secure with wooden toothpicks. Place chicken on lightly oiled barbecue and cook for 6–8 minutes each side or until chicken is tender and cooked.

**4** In a small pan, place chopped mango, garlic, golden syrup and sweet chilli sauce and cook, stirring, over a low heat for 4–5 minutes or until sauce thickens slightly. Serve with chicken.

| NUTRITIONAL VALUE PER SERVE | FAT 3.8 G | CARBOHYDRATE 5.7 G | PROTEIN 14.6 G |
|---|---|---|---|

# Seared tuna with roasted plum tomatoes

## INGREDIENTS

1 clove garlic, crushed
finely grated rind (zest) and juice of
    1 lime
½ cup (125 ml, 4 fl oz) olive oil
3 tablespoons chopped fresh
    rosemary
4 (145 g, 5 oz) tuna steaks,
    about 2 cm (1 in) thick
6 plum tomatoes, halved lengthways
1 red onion, halved and thinly sliced
    lengthways
salt and black pepper
extra olive oil for greasing
**serves 4**

PREPARATION TIME
20 minutes, plus
30 minutes marinating

COOKING TIME
30 minutes

1  Preheat barbecue to high. Preheat oven to 220°C (425°F, gas mark 7). In a large dish,
   combine garlic, lime rind, half the lime juice, 2 tablespoons of the oil and 1 tablespoon of
   the rosemary. Add the tuna and turn to coat evenly. Cover and refrigerate for 30 minutes.

2  Place the tomatoes and onion in a shallow ovenproof dish with the remaining rosemary.
   Drizzle with the remaining oil and season. Roast in the oven for 15–20 minutes, until
   tender and lightly browned.

3  Lightly oil barbecue grill bars. Place tuna on barbecue, cook for 4–5 minutes, turning once, or
   until golden. Serve with the tomatoes and onion, sprinkled with the remaining lime juice.

| NUTRITIONAL VALUE PER SERVE | FAT 21.6 G | CARBOHYDRATE 1.7 G | PROTEIN 5.1 G |
| --- | --- | --- | --- |

# Home-smoked trout

**INGREDIENTS**

125 g (4 oz) smoking chips
½ cup (125 ml, 4 fl oz) white wine
4 small rainbow trout, cleaned,
  with head and tail intact
1 tablespoon vegetable oil
3 red onions, thinly sliced
1 lemon, thinly sliced
8 sprigs dill
**serves 4**

1 Place smoking chips and wine in a large glass dish and stand for 1 hour.

2 Preheat covered barbecue to a low heat. Place smoking chips dish in barbecue over hot coals, cover barbecue with lid and heat for 5–10 minutes or until liquid is hot.

3 Place trout on a wire rack set in a roasting tin. Brush trout lightly with oil, then top with onions, lemon and dill. Place on rack in barbecue, cover and smoke for 15–20 minutes or until trout flakes when tested with fork.

PREPARATION TIME
**15 minutes, plus
1 hour standing**

COOKING TIME
**30 minutes**

NUTRITIONAL VALUE PER SERVE　　　FAT **4.8** G　　　CARBOHYDRATE **0.9** G　　　PROTEIN **19.4** G

# Char-grilled tuna with peach salsa

### INGREDIENTS

4 (about 180 g, 6 oz) tuna steaks
1 tablespoon olive oil
fresh coriander (cilantro) chopped
  to garnish
lime wedges to serve

*salsa*

3 ripe peaches, peeled, stoned
  and finely chopped
4 spring onions (green onions),
  finely chopped
1/2 yellow capsicum (pepper),
  finely chopped
juice of 1/2 lime
1 tablespoon chopped
  fresh coriander (cilantro)
black pepper

**serves 4**

1 In a small bowl, place peaches, spring onions (green onions), capsicum (pepper), lime juice, coriander (cilantro) and black pepper and mix well. Cover and refrigerate for 1 hour.

2 Preheat the barbecue to high. Brush tuna steaks with oil and season with pepper. Place on barbecue and cook for 3–5 minutes on each side, until flesh flakes when tested with a fork. Garnish with fresh coriander (cilantro) and serve with the lime wedges and peach salsa.

PREPARATION TIME
**20 minutes, plus
1 hour refrigeration**

COOKING TIME
**10 minutes**

NUTRITIONAL VALUE PER SERVE        FAT 3.8 G        CARBOHYDRATE 4.4 G        PROTEIN 6.7 G

# Seafood barbecue

## INGREDIENTS

4 tablespoons soy sauce
2 tablespoons honey
2 tablespoons tomato sauce
2 tablespoons sesame seeds
1 tablespoon lemon rind (zest),
  finely grated
375 g (12 oz) green prawns (shrimps),
  shelled and deveined, tails intact
250 g (8 oz) calamari (squid) rings
250 g (8 oz) boneless fish fillets,
  cut into thick strips
4 potatoes, thinly sliced
4 small tomatoes, halved
2 tablespoons chopped fresh thyme
freshly ground black pepper
lemon or lime wedges
**serves 4**

PREPARATION TIME
30 minutes, plus
20 minutes marinating

COOKING TIME
20 minutes

1 Preheat barbecue to a high heat. In a large shallow glass dish, place soy sauce, honey, tomato sauce, sesame seeds and lemon rind. Add prawns (shrimps), calamari (squid) and fish, toss to coat, cover and refrigerate for 20 minutes.

2 Sprinkle potatoes and tomatoes with thyme and black pepper to taste. Cook potatoes and tomatoes on a well-oiled barbecue plate for 10 minutes or until potatoes are crisp and tomatoes soft. Push vegetables to the side of the barbecue to keep warm.

3 Add seafood mixture to barbecue and cook, turning frequently, for 5 minutes or until cooked. Serve vegetables and seafood garnished with lemon or lime wedges.

| NUTRITIONAL VALUE PER SERVE | FAT 1.1 G | CARBOHYDRATE 6.9 G | PROTEIN 9.2 G |
|---|---|---|---|

# Lemongrass prawns

### INGREDIENTS

1 kg (2 lb) green prawns (shrimps)
3 stalks fresh lemongrass,
  finely chopped
2 spring onions (green onions),
  chopped
2 small fresh red chillies,
  finely chopped
2 cloves garlic, crushed
2 tablespoons finely grated
  fresh ginger
1 teaspoon shrimp paste
1 tablespoon brown sugar
$\frac{1}{2}$ cup (125 ml, 4 fl oz) coconut milk
**serves 4**

PREPARATION TIME
30 minutes, plus
3–4 hours marinating

COOKING TIME
15 minutes

1  Wash prawns, leaving shells and heads intact, and place in a
   shallow glass dish.

2  In a food processor or blender, place lemongrass, spring onions
   (green onions), chillies, garlic, ginger and shrimp paste and
   process until smooth. Add sugar and coconut milk and process to
   combine. Spoon mixture over prawns, toss to combine, cover and
   refrigerate for 3–4 hours.

3  Preheat barbecue to a high heat. Drain prawns, place on barbecue
   and cook, tossing gently, for 3–5 minutes until cooked.

| NUTRITIONAL VALUE PER SERVE | FAT 2.7 G | CARBOHYDRATE 1.7 G | PROTEIN 17.4 G |
|---|---|---|---|

# Coriander swordfish steaks

**INGREDIENTS**

125 g (4 oz) butter
2 tablespoons chopped
  fresh coriander (cilantro)
1 tablespoon parmesan, grated
4 swordfish steaks
1 tablespoon olive oil
4 courgettes (zucchini),
  cut into long slices
1 red capsicum (pepper), quartered
**serves 4**

1 Preheat barbecue to high. Cream the butter until soft and add the coriander (cilantro) and parmesan. Mix to combine, press into a butter pot and set aside.

2 Lightly oil barbecue grill bars. Brush fish steaks with oil, place on grill bars and cook 3–4 minutes each side according to thickness. Brush vegetables with oil and place on grill, cook for 3–4 minutes until golden. Serve vegetables and swordfish topped with a dollop of coriander butter.

PREPARATION TIME
**20 minutes**

COOKING TIME
**12 minutes**

NUTRITIONAL VALUE PER SERVE          FAT **11.8** G          CARBOHYDRATE **1.0** G          PROTEIN **9.8** G

# Barbecued vegetables

**INGREDIENTS**

300 g (10 oz) sweet potato, peeled
    and cut into 3 cm (1 in) thick slices
300 g (10 oz) pumpkin, peeled and
    cut into wedges
6 medium potatoes, halved
12 baby onions, whole
6 carrots, peeled
6 parsnips, peeled
6 baby beetroot, peeled
4 tablespoons olive oil
4 sprigs fresh thyme
4 sprigs fresh rosemary
**serves 6**

1  Preheat covered barbecue to medium.

2  Bring a large pan of water to the boil, add
   sweet potato, pumpkin and potatoes and cook
   for 10 minutes. Drain well.

3  Place sweet potato, pumpkin, potatoes, onions,
   carrots, parsnips and beetroot on a lightly oiled
   baking tray. Brush vegetables lightly with oil
   and scatter with sprigs of thyme and rosemary.

4  Place baking tray on rack in barbecue, cover
   barbecue with lid and cook for 40 minutes or
   until vegetables are tender.

PREPARATION TIME
**20 minutes**

COOKING TIME
**50 minutes**

NUTRITIONAL VALUE PER SERVE     FAT **2.6** G     CARBOHYDRATE **9.7** G     PROTEIN **1.8** G

# Pesto potato wedges

**INGREDIENTS**

4 medium-sized potatoes, peeled
2 tablespoons basil pesto
1 tablespoon olive oil
1 tablespoon water
60 g (2 oz) parmesan, grated
**serves 2–4**

**1** Preheat barbecue to high. Cut potatoes into wedges, rinse well and drain, then place in a large bowl. In a small bowl, combine basil pesto, olive oil and water. Pour over potatoes and toss to coat well. Place in a large foil dish in a single layer if possible.

**2** Cook over indirect heat in a covered barbecue for 40 minutes, turning after 20 minutes.

**3** Serve sprinkled with parmesan.

PREPARATION TIME
**15 minutes**

COOKING TIME
**40 minutes**

| NUTRITIONAL VALUE PER SERVE | FAT 10.4 G | CARBOHYDRATE 10.7 G | PROTEIN 6.3 G |

# Cajun barbecue corn

### INGREDIENTS

4 cobs sweet corn, halved
1 orange sweet potato,
   cut into 1 cm (¹/₄ in) thick slices
2 tablespoons butter, melted
*cajun spice mix*
1 teaspoon freshly ground
   black pepper
¹/₂ teaspoon chilli powder
1 teaspoon ground cumin
1 teaspoon ground coriander
   (cilantro)
2 teaspoons sweet paprika
**serves 4**

1 Preheat barbecue to a high heat.

2 In a small bowl, place black pepper, chilli powder, cumin, coriander (cilantro) and paprika and mix to combine.

3 Brush sweet corn and sweet potato with butter, sprinkle spice mix over vegetables. Place sweet corn and sweet potato on barbecue and cook, turning frequently, for 10–15 minutes or until vegetables are almost cooked.

PREPARATION TIME
**15 minutes**

COOKING TIME
**15 minutes**

| NUTRITIONAL VALUE PER SERVE | FAT 4.7 G | CARBOHYDRATE 15.2 G | PROTEIN 3.6 G |

# Glossary

**Al dente:** Italian term to describe pasta and rice that are cooked until tender but still firm to the bite.

**Bake blind:** to bake pastry cases without their fillings. Line the raw pastry case with greaseproof paper and fill with raw rice or dried beans to prevent collapsed sides and puffed base. Remove paper and fill 5 minutes before completion of cooking time.

**Baste:** to spoon hot cooking liquid over food at intervals during cooking to moisten and flavour it.

**Beat:** to make a mixture smooth with rapid and regular motions using a spatula, wire whisk or electric mixer; to make a mixture light and smooth by enclosing air.

**Beurre manié:** equal quantities of butter and flour mixed together to a smooth paste and stirred bit by bit into a soup, stew or sauce while on the heat to thicken. Stop adding when desired thickness results.

**Bind:** to add egg or a thick sauce to hold ingredients together when cooked.

**Blanch:** to plunge some foods into boiling water for less than a minute and immediately plunge into iced water. This is to brighten the colour of some vegetables and to remove skin from tomatoes and nuts.

**Blend:** to mix 2 or more ingredients thoroughly together; do not confuse with blending in an electric blender.

**Boil:** to cook in a liquid brought to boiling point and kept there.

**Boiling point:** when bubbles rise continually and break over the entire surface of the liquid, reaching a temperature of 100°C (212°F). In some cases food is held at this high temperature for a few seconds then heat is turned to low for slower cooking. See *simmer.*

**Bouquet garni:** a bundle of several herbs tied together with string for easy removal, placed into pots of stock, soups and stews for flavour. A few sprigs of fresh thyme, parsley and bay leaf are used. Can be purchased in sachet form for convenience.

**Caramelise:** to heat sugar in a heavy-based pan until it liquefies and develops a caramel colour. Vegetables such as blanched carrots and sautéed onions may be sprinkled with sugar and caramelised.

**Chill:** to place in the refrigerator or stir over ice until cold.

**Clarify:** to make a liquid clear by removing sediments and impurities. To melt fat and remove any sediment.

**Coat:** to dust or roll food items in flour to cover the surface before the food is cooked. Also, to coat in flour, egg and breadcrumbs.

**Cool:** to stand at room temperature until some or all heat is removed, eg cool a little, cool completely.

**Cream:** to make creamy and fluffy by working the mixture with the back of a wooden spoon; usually refers to creaming butter and sugar or margarine. May also be done with an electric mixer.

**Croutons:** small cubes of bread, toasted or fried, used as an addition to salads or as a garnish to soups and stews.

**Crudités:** raw vegetable sticks served with a dipping sauce.

**Crumb:** to coat foods in flour, egg and breadcrumbs to form a protective coating for foods which are fried. Also adds flavour and texture and enhances appearance.

**Cube:** to cut into small pieces with six even sides, eg cubes of meat.

**Cut in:** to combine fat, such as butter or shortening, and flour using 2 knives scissor-fashion or a pastry blender, to make pastry.

**Deglaze:** to dissolve dried-out cooking juices left on the base and sides of a roasting dish or frying pan. Add a little water, wine or stock, scrape and stir over heat until dissolved. Resulting liquid is used to make a flavoursome gravy or added to a sauce or casserole.

**Degrease:** to skim fat from the surface of cooking liquids, eg stocks, soups, casseroles.

**Dice:** to cut into small cubes.

**Dredge:** to heavily coat with icing sugar, sugar, flour or cornflour.

**Dressing:** a mixture added to completed dishes to add moisture and flavour, eg salads, cooked vegetables.

**Drizzle:** to pour in a fine thread-like stream moving over a surface.

**Egg wash:** beaten egg with milk or water used to brush over pastry, bread dough or biscuits to give a sheen and golden brown colour.

**Essence:** a strong flavouring liquid, usually made by distillation. Only a few drops are needed to flavour.

**Fillet:** a piece of prime meat, fish or poultry which is boneless or has all bones removed.

**Flake:** to separate cooked fish into flakes, removing any bones and skin, using 2 forks.

**Flame:** to ignite warmed alcohol over food or to pour into a pan with food, ignite, then serve.

**Flute:** to make decorative indentations around the pastry rim before baking.

**Fold in:** combining of a light, whisked or creamed mixture with other ingredients. Add a portion of the other ingredients at a time and mix using a gentle circular motion, over and under the mixture so that air will not be lost. Use a metal spoon or spatula.

**Glaze:** to brush or coat food with a liquid that will give the finished product a glossy appearance, and on baked products, a golden brown colour.

**Grease:** to rub the surface of a metal or heatproof dish with oil or fat, to prevent the food from sticking.

**Herbed butter:** softened butter mixed with finely chopped fresh herbs and re-chilled. Used to serve on grilled meats and fish.

**Hors d'oeuvre:** small savoury foods served as an appetiser, popularly known today as 'finger food'.

**Infuse:** to steep foods in a liquid until the liquid absorbs their flavour.

**Joint:** to cut poultry and game into serving pieces by dividing at the joint.

**Julienne:** to cut some food, eg vegetables and processed meats, into fine strips the length of matchsticks. Used in salads or as a garnish to cooked dishes.

**Knead:** to work a yeast dough in a pressing, stretching and folding motion with the heel of the hand until smooth and elastic to develop the gluten strands. Non-yeast doughs should be lightly and quickly handled as gluten development is not desired.

**Line:** to cover the inside of a baking tin with paper for the easy removal of the cooked product from the baking tin.

**Macerate:** to stand fruit in a syrup, liqueur or spirit to give added flavour.

**Marinade:** a flavoured liquid, into which food is placed for some time to give it flavour and to tenderise. Marinades include an acid ingredient such as vinegar or wine, oil and seasonings.

**Mask:** to evenly cover cooked food portions with a sauce, mayonnaise or savoury jelly.

**Pan-fry:** to fry foods in a small amount of fat or oil, sufficient to coat the base of the pan.

**Parboil:** to boil until partially cooked. The food is then finished by some other method.

**Pare:** to peel the skin from vegetables and fruit. 'Peel' is the popular term but 'pare' is the name given to the knife used; paring knife.

**Pit:** to remove stones or seeds from olives, cherries, dates.

**Pith:** the white lining between the rind and flesh of oranges, grapefruit and lemons.

**Pitted:** the olives, cherries, dates etc. with the stone removed, eg purchase pitted dates.

**Poach:** to simmer gently in enough hot liquid to almost cover the food so its shape will be retained.

**Pound:** to flatten meats with a meat mallet; to reduce to a paste or small particles with a mortar and pestle.

**Simmer:** to cook in liquid just below boiling point at about 96°C (205°F) with small bubbles rising gently to the surface.

**Skim:** to remove fat or froth from the surface of simmering food.

**Stock:** the liquid produced when meat, poultry, fish or vegetables have been simmered in water to extract the flavour. Used as a base for soups, sauces, casseroles etc. Convenience stock products are available.

**Sweat:** to cook sliced onions or vegetables in a small amount of butter in a covered pan over low heat, to soften them and release flavour without colouring.

# Conversions

Measurements differ from country to country, so it's important to understand what the differences are. This Measurements Guide gives you simple 'at-a-glance' information for using the recipes in this book, wherever you may be.

Cooking is not an exact science – minor variations in measurements won't make a difference to your cooking.

### EQUIPMENT

There is a difference in the size of measuring cups used internationally, but the difference is minimal (only 2–3 teaspoons). We use the standard metric measurements in our recipes:

1 teaspoon.....5 ml   1 tablespoon.....20 ml
½ cup.....125 ml   1 cup.....250 ml
4 cups.....1 litre

Measuring cups come in sets of one cup (250 ml), ½ cup (125 ml), ⅓ cup (80 ml) and ¼ cup (60 ml). Use these for measuring liquids and certain dry ingredients.

Measuring spoons come in a set of four and should be used for measuring dry and liquid ingredients.

When using cup or spoon measures, always make them level (unless the recipe indicates otherwise).

### DRY VERSUS WET INGREDIENTS

While this system of measures is consistent for liquids, it's more difficult to quantify dry ingredients. For instance, one level cup equals: 200 g of brown sugar; 210 g of castor sugar; and 110 g of icing sugar.

When measuring dry ingredients such as flour, don't push the flour down or shake it into the cup. It is best just to spoon the flour in until it reaches the desired amount. When measuring liquids, use a clear vessel indicating metric levels.

Always use medium eggs (55–60 g) when eggs are required in a recipe.

### OVEN

Your oven should always be at the right temperature before placing the food in it to be cooked. Note that if your oven doesn't have a fan you may need to cook food for a little longer.

### MICROWAVE

It is difficult to give an exact cooking time for microwave cooking. It is best to watch what you are cooking closely to monitor its progress.

### STANDING TIME

Many foods continue to cook when you take them out of the oven or microwave. If a recipe states that the food needs to 'stand' after cooking, be sure not to overcook the dish.

### CAN SIZES

The can sizes available in your supermarket or grocery store may not be the same as specified in the recipe. Don't worry if there is a small variation in size – it's unlikely to make a difference to the end result.

| dry | | liquids | |
|---|---|---|---|
| metric (grams) | imperial (ounces) | metric (millilitres) | imperial (fluid ounces) |
| | | 30 ml | 1 fl oz |
| 30 g | 1 oz | 60 ml | 2 fl oz |
| 60 g | 2 oz | 90 ml | 3 fl oz |
| 90 g | 3 oz | 100 ml | 3 1/2 fl oz |
| 100 g | 3 1/2 oz | 125 ml | 4 fl oz |
| 125 g | 4 oz | 150 ml | 5 fl oz |
| 150 g | 5 oz | 190 ml | 6 fl oz |
| 185 g | 6 oz | 250 ml | 8 fl oz |
| 200 g | 7 oz | 300 ml | 10 fl oz |
| 250 g | 8 oz | 500 ml | 16 fl oz |
| 280 g | 9 oz | 600 ml | 20 fl oz  (1 pint)* |
| 315 g | 10 oz | 1000 ml (1 litre) | 32 fl oz |
| 330 g | 11 oz | | |
| 370 g | 12 oz | | |
| 400 g | 13 oz | | |
| 440 g | 14 oz | | |
| 470 g | 15 oz | | |
| 500 g | 16 oz (1 lb) | | |
| 750 g | 24 oz (1 1/2 lb) | | |
| 1000 g (1 kg) | 32 oz (2 lb) | *Note: an American pint is 16 fl oz. | |

| cooking temperatures | °C (celsius) | °F (fahrenheit) | gas mark |
|---|---|---|---|
| very slow | 120 | 250 | 1/2 |
| slow | 150 | 300 | 2 |
| moderately slow | 160 | 315 | 2–3 |
| moderate | 180 | 350 | 4 |
| moderately hot | 190 | 375 | 5 |
| | 200 | 400 | 6 |
| hot | 220 | 425 | 7 |
| very hot | 230 | 450 | 8 |
| | 240 | 475 | 9 |
| | 250 | 500 | 10 |

# Index